Anacondas

Leo Statts

abdopublishing.com

Published by Abdo Zoom™, PO Box 398166, Minneapolis, Minnesota 55439. Copyright © 2017 by Abdo Consulting Group, Inc. International copyrights reserved in all countries. No part of this book may be reproduced in any form without written permission from the publisher. Abdo Zoom™ is a trademark and logo of Abdo Consulting Group, Inc.

Printed in the United States of America, North Mankato, Minnesota
062016
092016

Cover Photo: Shutterstock Images
Interior Photos: Shutterstock Images, 1, 5, 8; Michael Meshcheryakov/Shutterstock Images, 4; Patrick K. Campbell/Shutterstock Images, 7 (top); Wayne Lynch/Glow Images, 7 (bottom); Tom Brakefield/Thinkstock, 9; iStockphoto, 10–11, 17; Red Line Editorial, 11, 20 (left), 20 (right), 21 (left), 21 (right); Matthew Cole/Shutterstock Images, 12; Yoshiharu Sekino/Science Source, 14–15; Gowri Varanashi/Shutterstock Images, 18; Vadim Petrakov/Shutterstock Images, 19

Editor: Brienna Rossiter
Series Designer: Madeline Berger
Art Direction: Dorothy Toth

Publisher's Cataloging-in-Publication Data
Names: Statts, Leo, author.
Title: Anacondas / by Leo Statts.
Description: Minneapolis, MN : Abdo Zoom, [2017] | Series: Rain forest animals | Includes bibliographical references and index.
Identifiers: LCCN 2016941132 | ISBN 9781680791921 (lib. bdg.) | ISBN 9781680793604 (ebook) | ISBN 9781680794496 (Read-to-me ebook)
Subjects: LCSH: Anacondas--Juvenile literature.
Classification: DDC 597.96--dc23
LC record available at http://lccn.loc.gov/2016941132

Table of Contents

Anacondas

Anacondas are
big snakes.

They weigh more than any other snake. There are four types of anacondas.

5

Green anacondas and yellow anacondas are the most common.

Green anacondas are the biggest.

Yellow anacondas are smaller.

7

Body

An anaconda's eyes are on top of its head.

So are its nostrils.

This helps it see and breathe in the water.

Habitat

Anacondas live in South America. Some live in swamps or streams. Others live in rain forests. They may even live in trees.

Where anacondas live

Food

Anacondas eat anything they can swallow. Fish and birds are common food. They also eat **reptiles**.

Anacondas squeeze
their food to kill it.

Sometimes they hold
it under water.

Life Cycle

Anacondas are born live.
Most are born in the water.

They can swim right away.

They shed their skin
each time they grow.

They live for approximately ten years.

Average Length

A green anaconda is shorter than a school bus.

26 ft   35 ft

Average Weight

A green anaconda is heavier than a refrigerator.

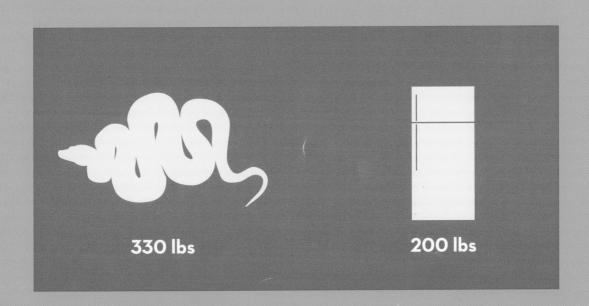

330 lbs   200 lbs

Glossary

rain forest - a tropical woodland where it rains a lot.

reptile - a cold-blooded animal with scales. They typically lay eggs.

shed - when hair or skin falls off an animal's body.

stream - a small, flowing body of water.

swamp - wet land that is filled with trees, plants, or both.

Booklinks

For more information
on anacondas, please visit
booklinks.abdopublishing.com

 In on Animals!

Learn even more with the Abdo Zoom
Animals database. Check out
abdozoom.com for more information.

Index